Original title:
Beneath the Christmas Tree's Glow

Copyright © 2024 Creative Arts Management OÜ
All rights reserved.

Author: Finn Donovan
ISBN HARDBACK: 978-9916-90-882-2
ISBN PAPERBACK: 978-9916-90-883-9

Lanterns of Love on Frosted Night

In the corner, cats play tag,
Tinsel flying, oh what a drag!
Uncle Joe spills his drink with care,
While Grandma laughs and pulls her hair.

The cookies vanish, hardly a trace,
Mysterious crumbs all over the place.
Squeaky toys for the kids abound,
While dogs plot mischief, making rounds.

The Promise of Peace in Soft Light

Dad's snoring softly, what a delight,
Wrapped in his sweater, oh so tight.
The lights twinkle like fireflies near,
While Aunt May claims she's had too much cheer.

The fruitcake sits with a menacing grin,
Declaring holiday madness to begin.
Cousin Tim's rocking the tree so low,
It's a wonder it hasn't tossed him in tow.

Cradled by the Flicker of Wishes

Playing charades, what a sight to see,
Mom thinks she's a tree, Dad's a bee.
With giggles echoing through the hall,
Jacob's convinced he's a reindeer tall.

Grandpa tells stories, each one a bore,
While the kids sneak candy right from the floor.
Confetti from last year's party appears,
A confounding mix of laughter and tears.

A Symphony of Love and Light

Wrapping gifts turns into a fight,
With tape and ribbons tangled just right.
Sisters squabble, but there's no real hate,
As the dog sneaks off with the best plate.

Cheers arise for the dinner parade,
Toasting to moments that simply won't fade.
Laughter and joy, that's the best part,
As we light up the season right from the heart.

Shadows in the Festive Glow

In the corner, a cat sits tight,
Chasing ornaments in the night.
The lights blink, a curious sight,
As the dog dreams of a snowball fight.

Grandma's cookies, a secret treat,
A flour explosion, oh what a feat!
Flour on her nose, what a funny greet,
Who knew baking could taste so sweet?

The Magic of Unseen Dreams

Ornaments swinging, a dance they make,
A sparkling reindeer takes a break.
Mice plotting mischief, for goodness' sake,
While stockings wish for a bellyache.

Tinsel tangles in a yarny mess,
The puppy chews without distress.
Shrugging it off, we wear the dress,
Laughter erupts, oh, what a bless!

Garlands and Glitter

The elf on the shelf, with a smirk so sly,
Is it magic or a curious lie?
He's swapped the cookies for broccoli, oh my!
Santa's diet? I question why!

Sparkles flying, like disco balls,
With socks on the floor, the merriment calls.
A slip, a trip, oh how it enthralls,
As laughter bounces off frosty walls.

Heartbeats Alight

Presents wrapped in paper so bright,
But one holds a tickle, what a fright!
A bear that giggles, oh what delight,
Who knew gifts could be such a sight?

A snowman inside the heated room,
With jolly laughter that starts to zoom.
He tells jokes with festive perfume,
And spreads happiness like a flower in bloom.

Echoes of Laughter in the Stillness

The jingle bells clash, a hilarious tune,
While grandma's losing the air from her balloon.
A turkey escapes, causing a swoon,
And uncles pose like stars on the moon.

Under the mistletoe, kisses go astray,
As aunties giggle and children play.
Joy spreads around like a bright cabaret,
In the magic of laughter, we bask today.

Whispers of Winter's Warm Embrace

The snowman's nose is a carrot bite,
But he's in trouble, it just won't stayight.
The cat thinks it's a game to attack,
As he launches an ambush, ready to snack.

The fire crackles with a joyful cheer,
While socks disappear, oh dear, oh dear!
Grandma's baking, but forgot the pie,
We'll feast on cookies—oh me, oh my!

Enchanted Shadows in Festive Light

The lights twinkle like disco balls,
While uncle dances, and nearly falls.
Minced pies vanish, just like last year,
Oops, spilled the eggnog—let's all cheer!

The elf on the shelf is plotting his scheme,
While the dog's dreaming of a big steak dream.
Families gather, with laughter galore,
Proving once more, less is not more!

Twinkling Dreams Wrapped in Memory

Each gift is wrapped like a burrito,
With bows like hats on a sleepy sheepto.
The kids scream with glee when they see,
A toy that makes noise—oh joy and glee!

The wrapping paper flies in quick bursts,
As dad reconsiders his "gift-unwrapping" thirst.
A surprise awaits, with glitter and giggles,
While mom just rolls her eyes at his wiggles.

The Magic Hidden in Evergreen Hugs

A wreath on the door, slightly askew,
It fell off again, we knew it would too!
The ornaments dance on the tip of a limb,
While the dog tries to help with an innocent whim.

A tree that leans—oh what a sight,
With baubles dancing through the night.
As laughter erupts in a jolly roar,
It's the season of chaos, who could ask for more?

Lighted Paths of Joyful Discovery

Under twinkling stars so bright,
Cats chase shadows in delight.
Gift wrap battles, tape in tangles,
A prank pulls laughs, and giggles wrangle.

Cookies vanish in a blink,
Leaving crumbs to make us think.
A dance with lights that spark and flash,
A moment's joy in silly clash.

Gifted Moments in Glowing Tranquility

Stockings hung, with wishes near,
But what's that smell? Oh dear, oh dear!
Uncle Joe, the cookie thief,
Nods off, still clutching his belief.

Ornaments swirl in boozy cheer,
While cousins spin tales we all hear.
With laughter bright, and drinks in hand,
We all toast to our merry band.

Shimmering Hues of Peaceful Nights

The fire crackles, logs go pop,
Grandma's snoring, should we stop?
A gentle nudge, she rocks with glee,
As everyone hums 'Jingle Me!'

Furry friends, all wrapped in bows,
Sneaky paws and playful woes.
In the bustle, hugs unfold,
Mirth and laughter, tales retold.

Holding Close What the Heart Admires

Pine-scented air, a cozy wrap,
With mismatched socks, we're all a chap.
The tree leans, like a tipsy friend,
Sparkling lights, on mischief we depend.

Sipping cocoa, marshmallows float,
As Dad's tight shirt tries to gloat.
Snickered gifts, each one a jest,
Bringing joy that feels the best.

The Beauty of Gifts Given Freely

A package wrapped with cheer,
But inside, just a sock, oh dear!
The cat jumps high, oh what a sight,
As I unwrap with all my might.

A tie so bright, it blinds my eyes,
It's perfect for my uncle's pies!
The joy of gifts, so mixed and strange,
Yet laughter is the sweetest change.

Echoes of Joy in Glowing Reflections

The lights are twinkling, what a mess,
Why's granddad dancing in a dress?
Flashing bulbs and cookies burnt,
On silly tales, our hearts will churn.

The laughter bounces off the walls,
While grandpa's snoring still enthralls.
Each echo mingles, bright and clear,
With giggles dancing, we hold dear.

The Harmony of Hearts in Unison

We sing off-key, our voices clash,
Mom throws her hands up, what a bash!
Yet in this chaos, love does swell,
In harmony, we laugh so well.

The dog joins in, howls on the floor,
As we all cringe and beg for more.
Each note is funny, out of place,
But joy's the song we all embrace.

Cherished Moments in the Glow of Hope

The wrapping paper flies around,
With giggles mixed in every sound.
A gift of socks? A book? Oh wait!
The dog just ate grandpa's plate!

Yet hope shines bright as pine trees sway,
In silly blunders, we find our way.
Each moment glows with laughter's spark,
As joy ignites the brightest mark.

Flickers of Joy

The lights are bright, but so are we,
A dance of socks, quite slippery.
The cat leaps high, what a sight,
Chasing shadows, oh, what a fright!

Cookies left out, the milk spilled wide,
Santa's got nothing on this ride.
Gifts wrapped tight in colorful paper,
Who knew tape could cause such caper?

Timeless as Ever

Last year's sweater, it's still a hit,
Knitted with love, but what a fit!
Grandma laughs, and so do we,
Where's the fashion police, you see?

Mismatched socks and a serious grin,
Who wears the turkey? Let the feast begin!
Dancing around with hot cocoa's swirl,
Another round, let's give it a whirl!

Hidden Treasures of the Season's Heart

Beneath the bramble, what's that smell?
A fruitcake from last year, oh well!
With every bite, a laugh or two,
Hidden treasures, it's all so true!

A mystery gift, what will it be?
A rubber chicken? Oh, make it three!
Laughter bubbles, wrapped in delight,
Christmas chaos, oh what a sight!

A Tapestry of Smiles and Embrace

Uncle Joe spins tales, oh what a mess,
Each one crazier, we must confess!
A reindeer on skates, can you believe?
Everyone chuckles, we can't reprieve!

Baking mishaps, flour in our hair,
Gingerbread houses that just don't compare.
Laughter stitches our hearts so tight,
A tapestry bright, in this joyful night!

Gliding Through a Winter Wonderland

Sliding down hills on a trashcan lid,
Watch out for trees, oh what a bid!
Snowball shenanigans, laughter rings,
Who knew winter could bring such things?

The snowman wobbles, eyes on his nose,
In a scarf a bit too big, I suppose.
We cheer and tumble, all in good fun,
Gliding through chaos, the day is won!

The Stillness Before the Unfolding

In the quiet of the night,
Stockings hung with hopes so bright,
Elves are sleeping, dreaming deep,
While Santa checks his list of sheep.

Crackers popped and hats askew,
Grandpa snores, it's nothing new,
Cookies vanish in a flash,
While kids retreat with a big stash.

Cats attack the twinkling lights,
As dogs chase shadows, what a sight!
The tree seems ready for its show,
With tinsel stuck on kids below.

Laughter bubbles, jokes abound,
As wrapping paper hits the ground,
The night is wild, a joyful spree,
In our home, pure jubilee!

Surrender to the Season's Charm

Ribbons curling, colors bright,
Uncle Joe is in a fright,
Socks that smell of holiday fun,
Who knew baking could weigh a ton?

Mistletoe, a sneaky kiss,
Granny's recipe - pure bliss,
Yet her cake is set ablaze,
All the family in a daze.

Snowmen wear the neighbor's hat,
And stray cats get into that,
Our secret stash was found at last,
But now it's gone, Christmas blast!

Flavored candy canes surprise,
Stuck in hair and squinting eyes,
Jingle bells on everyone,
Season's play has just begun!

Tales of Wonder in Secret Spaces

Behind the couch, a toy brigade,
Gathering dust, plans well laid,
Jokes and laughter fill the air,
While squirrels plot without a care.

A treasure hunt beneath the bed,
Old lollipops and candy spread,
Maps they drew with crayons bright,
Discoveries made in pure delight.

Invisible friends join the game,
It's all so silly, yet the same,
Under holo-glow they scheme,
Turning the night into a dream.

Tales of wonder softly weave,
Magic flows that none believe,
With giggles echoing all around,
In all the secrets we have found!

Soft Hues of Nostalgia Glimmering

Colors dance in playful glee,
Ornaments whisper 'look at me',
Back to when we were much small,
Just too shy at the grand ball.

Pinecones roll, a game ensues,
While mom crochets in her shoes,
Dad's stuck under the branches thick,
Is it real, or just a trick?

Every gift contains a lore,
Scratchy sweaters, knick-knack score,
Family quirks are on full show,
Tales erupt like winter snow.

Yet through all the chance and cheer,
We find the laughter, shed the fear,
Moments pass, but joy stays bright,
Underneath this festive light!

Harmonies of the Season Unfold

Tinsel tangled in the hair,
Lights that flicker, quite a scare.
Cookies vanish, oh so fast,
We'll be baking, what a blast!

Reindeer games up on the roof,
With my cat, there goes my proof.
Santa's list, I made it twice,
Could he take a little slice?

Stockings stuffed with oddities,
Lumps of coal and potpourris.
In the chaos, laughter rings,
While we dance and joyfully sing.

Elves in mismatched, silly socks,
Making toys with squeaky knocks.
Under all the shiny scenes,
We find laughter in routines.

Glimmers of Hope Amidst the Chill

Snowflakes swirl, a frosty dance,
As grandpa's snoring steals the chance.
Mugs of cocoa by the fire,
Sipping wildly, my attire!

Gifts wrapped oddly, some with flair,
What's this? A sock - oh, where's the pair?
Antlers on the dog we put,
He chews them off, that silly mutt!

Giggling kids with sticky hands,
Making snowmen in the lands.
Laughter echoes, loud and clear,
As we make snowballs, full of cheer.

Snowball fights and feigned defeat,
Victory claimed, dodging feet.
Underneath it all, we'd find,
Joyful moments intertwined.

A Cascade of Light in the Stillness

Lights aglow, a sparkling spree,
Mom's caught dancing, you should see!
Her moves are wild, it's quite a scene,
Her kitchen's now a disco dream!

Garlands hung with hasty care,
Watch out for that chair - beware!
Trip and tangle, fall with grace,
We laugh at how we lose our place.

Nuts and fruitcake, what a treat,
No one wants that festive feat.
Still we chew, with faces grim,
As we celebrate on a whim.

Twinkling bright, the evenings laugh,
Board game battles, we're a gaffe.
Cheers to all in festive cheer,
With goofy fun that brings us near.

Breath of Winter in the Air

Winter's breath brings slush and sliding,
Pass the hot cocoa, crazy riding.
Snowmen sporting hats askew,
What's this? A nose, a lettuce too!

Furry boots and scarves so long,
When we sing, it's still quite wrong.
Voices crack like brittle ice,
But we sing out, not thinking twice.

Pies are baking, what a smell,
Hope we don't burn them - oh, as well!
Grandma claims her secret spice,
But we taste it, oh how nice!

So here's to joy and merry cheer,
With silly hats and hearty beer.
Let's embrace all laughter's glee,
This winter's fun beneath the spree.

Midnight Conversations Among the Ornaments

Baubles chat about the year,
While tinsel teeters, full of cheer.
Ribbons gossip, sharing tales,
Of squirrels stealing their shiny scales.

Candles wink with nervous glee,
As elves dance wild, who can it be?
Stars are snickering overhead,
While the floor's strewn with crumbs of bread.

Mice with hats claim their own space,
As angels blush, now out of place.
A nutcracker whispers with a grin,
"Who knew the fun would start at ten?"

Toys awake, revolt begins,
Santa's sleigh is filled with sins.
A rubber duck quacks out a joke,
As night unfolds and laughter spoke.

The Dance of Shadows and Lights

Twinkling bulbs begin their show,
As shadows leap, a lively flow.
Elves in corners, doing the twist,
In a battle with a rogue mist.

Garlands swing with jolly cheer,
While ornaments eye the mugs of beer.
A Santa doll does the macarena,
While candles melt, creating a scene-a.

Snowmen laugh, have lost their hats,
As kittens chase the playful bats.
The moon peeks in, a curious guest,
Watching silliness, we're all blessed.

Underneath the glow tonight,
Everyone's gathered, what a sight!
A merry chaos fills the air,
As laughter bubbles everywhere!

Heartfelt Memories in Winter's Cloak

The snowman's nose is on the fritz,
As kids outshine the holiday blitz.
Mistletoe hangs all askew,
While grandma's cookies—oops!—went blue.

Pinecones whisper secrets loud,
As reindeer prance, claiming a crowd.
A bear with mittens, quite befuddled,
Caught in ribbons, gets thoroughly cuddled.

Frosty sips from cocoa mugs,
While nutcrackers do the jitterbugs.
Each memory a cheerful song,
In quirky ways, we all belong.

The silly hat's the star tonight,
In laughter's glow, we feel so right.
With every poke, the joy will grow,
In this winter tale, the fun will flow.

Whispers of Magic, Flickering Bright

Magic sparkles in the air,
As fairies twirl without a care.
Gingerbread men start to flee,
As icing smiles evoke great glee.

A wobbly tree's bending low,
With garlands tangled in a show.
Elves are plotting with their flair,
To outwit Santa, if they dare.

Toys are trading sly, sweet jokes,
While mistletoe plays on the hoax.
The angel winks, then takes a spin,
As holiday antics soon begin.

With every flicker, mischief flows,
In every corner, laughter grows.
A night of wonders, pure delight,
In the glow that shines so bright.

Echoing Dreams Beneath Soft Glimmers

Laughter echoes in the space,
As reindeer dance in silly grace.
The cookies vanish, crumbs galore,
Santa's stuck, we can't ignore.

A cat in tinsel, what a sight,
Chasing shadows, pure delight.
Mistletoe hangs, we brace for fun,
Awkward kisses, everyone!

Snowflakes fall like feathery dreams,
Hot cocoa spills, oh the screams!
Elf hats wobble, the jokes they weave,
This merry chaos, who wouldn't believe?

Stockings stuffed with oddities bright,
Like Auntie's fruitcake, a frightful bite!
Yet in this madness, love does flow,
With giggles, cheers, beneath twinkling glow.

The Radiance of Togetherness and Cheer

Gathered here, we twirl and spin,
In our hearts, the fun begins.
Grandpa's snoring, what a dear,
His nap the highlight of the year!

Lights flicker like a dance of glee,
While doggy tries to climb the tree.
The ornaments crash, oh what a sound,
But laughter's our joy, all around.

Wrapping paper's torn with flair,
With chaos raining everywhere.
Uncle's jokes, they land with thud,
Yet smiles bloom like bulbs in mud.

We raise a toast with glasses bright,
To family, laughter, and sheer delight.
With every cheer, we find our place,
In this warm, silly, loving space.

Silent Whispers of Winter's Embrace

Snowmen wobble in silent pose,
As sleds zoom past with squeals and prose.
The air is filled with much delight,
Snowball fights and snowflakes white.

Whispers lift on frosty breath,
As cookies tease a nearing death.
The dog hides gifts, a sneaky ploy,
While kids gang up on a frozen toy.

Jingle bells ring with a quirky beat,
As everyone dances, right on their feet.
The awkward shimmy, the sliding slide,
In winter's party, we all collide.

With giggles ringing loud and clear,
We savor moments filled with cheer.
For in this season, we become,
A silly family, all in one.

Secrets Wrapped in Twinkling Lights

Presents piled in a tangled heap,
What lies within? Our secrets to keep!
Giggles echo as we pry,
As chorus voices croon nearby.

Mismatched socks in the festive stash,
A grandma's joke makes the young hearts flash.
A gift that squeaks, a chord that rings,
In weird surprises, joy springs.

Dancers twirl in glittery flair,
Even the cat jumps up to share.
Tinsel tumbles, garlands fall,
Who knew that laughter could bind us all?

So here we are, with ears adorned,
Sipping cider, spirits warmed.
In this merry mess, with all our might,
We share our secrets wrapped in light.

Frosted Whispers and Heartfelt Greetings

Presents stacked in a wobbly tower,
A cat has claimed the topmost flower.
Tinsel tangled in a jolly twist,
Mom's yelling, 'Who wrapped that in mist?'

Lights are blinking in a silly spree,
Dad tripped over a chipmunk marquee.
Cookies missing, oh where could they be?
The dog grins wide, as happy as can be.

Joy Untangled in Radiant Glow

Elves are giggling, stuck in the wreath,
One lost a shoe, can you believe?
Snowflakes falling with a delicate dance,
Neighbors peeking, hoping for a chance.

Grandma's fruitcake is a sight to see,
The reindeer ate half, now who's guilty?
Ribbons swirling in chaotic cheer,
We laugh so hard we can barely steer.

The Dance of Festive Flurries

Snowmen wobble, a lopsided sight,
Froze our noses in delight so bright.
The kids chuckle with snowballs in hand,
While slipping and sliding, they form a band.

A squirrel steals a shiny red bow,
While we all giggle, 'Oh no, not so!'
Hot cocoa spills, it's a marshmallow fight,
Joyously messy, the world feels just right.

Memories Wrapped in Crimson and Gold

Wrapping paper scattered, a colorful mess,
Grandpa's been napping; oh, what a stress!
The tree is leaning, it's seen better days,
But we'll never forget these festive plays.

Jingle bells jingling, slightly out of tune,
A cat sounds the alarm; it's almost noon!
We all raise a glass to this silly crew,
Cheers to the joy and the laughter, too!

Joys Hidden Within the Greenery

In needles sharp, the secrets hide,
A rogue squirrel plays, with festive pride.
He leaps and bounds, a real acrobat,
While ornaments giggle, imagine that!

Upon the floor, a gift unwrapped,
A jigsaw puzzle, but none are clapped.
We laugh and squabble for pieces lost,
Over tiny parts, we pay the cost.

Eggnog spills, what a comical scene,
A cat in a bow, still looking keen.
She twirls and sways, oh what a sight,
Her puzzled meow brings sheer delight!

With cookies left, the crumbs all spread,
A sprinkle of sugar and a dash of dread.
For if you bite too hard, beware the crunch,
A fruity explosion, best not for lunch!

Mirth Unwrapped: Tales of Delight

A box wrapped tight, I want to peep,
But the tape's so strong, my fingers creep.
In laughter trapped, I bring my might,
As family giggles at my little fight.

A fortune cookie, oh what a mess,
The fortune reads, "Your socks, who knows best?"
We all burst out, hold our feet in glee,
As none have matched since last year's spree.

The dog finds joy in ribbon's long chase,
He tangles himself, then stops to face.
With a mighty bark, he springs to go,
But alas! He's stuck, what a funny show!

In the corner, a fruitcake stands alone,
Its weighty mass could build a throne.
We tease and poke, then take a bite,
The taste of laughter, pure delight!

Frosted Wishes and Candlelight Dreams

Under the lights, we start to sway,
With clumsy moves in our holiday ballet.
The grandma whirls, a sight to behold,
While warm apple cider matches her bold.

On the table, cookies stacked so high,
But the kids miscount and reach for the pie.
Sugar-fueled giggles fill the air,
As frosting fights start, with careless flair!

We tell old tales of snowball fights,
Where socks were used for winter nights.
With laughter ringing through the hall,
Each frosted wish turns into a brawl!

A candle flickers, nearly falls down,
The cat gives chase, now what's that sound?
With paws in the air, she takes a leap,
And into the pies, a real comic sweep!

Radiance of Family Gathered

Gathered around, the couch holds tight,
As Uncle Joe cracks jokes all night.
With silly puns that make us groan,
We find new reasons to moan and drone.

A game of charades turns into a mess,
With grandpa's moves, we can only guess.
He flails his arms, a chicken in flight,
We roll on the floor, what a funny sight!

Presents exchanged, but whispers so sly,
"It's definitely not for you," they cry.
As they shake and rattle, we can't resist,
Finding joy in things that don't exist!

The tree's aglow, but certainly clear,
That family's laughter's the best souvenir.
For fun and cheer, we all bestow,
Radiance brightens each heart's overflow!

Wrapped in Love

Presents piled high, oh what a scene,
Boxes that jiggle, you know what I mean!
Ribbons like snakes, twist and twirl,
Who knew joy could spiral and swirl?

Cats in the chaos, they pounce for a peek,
Wrapping paper shreds, what a cheek!
Laughter erupts with each furry attack,
Christmas spirit won't hold us back!

Uniting Hearts

Cookies are baking, the cookie monster's feast,
Mom's secret stash, oh, to say the least!
A sprinkle of chaos, flour in the air,
Family's infectious laughter everywhere!

Socks that disappear, where do they roam?
Silent night? Please, not in this home!
Our hearts are united, each silly prank,
Makes memories more precious than gold in the bank!

The Glow of Generosity's Spirit

Gifts for the neighbor, all wrapped with a grin,
But oops! There's a cat, what a furry spin!
In search of our kindness, he leaves us a hair,
'Tis the season to share—not the cat's despair!

Labels all mixed, where's Uncle Joe's hat?
Is this one for Grandma, or did I gift the cat?
Cheerful mishaps, we'll laugh till we drop,
Generosity blossoms, who knew it could flop?

Beneath Branches of Whimsy and Cheer

Decorations are tangled, mistletoe's askew,
Kissing the air, but who kissed the shoe?
Twinkle lights flicker, dance with delight,
Whimsy spills laughter, all through the night!

Children rejoice as the snowflakes fall,
Building their forts, it's a free-for-all!
While adults sip cocoa, with marshmallows galore,
Hilarity happens—what's behind that door?

Enchanted Moments in December's Embrace

Snowmen rising tall, with a carrot so grand,
But wait! Is that snow? Or a snowy handstand?
Cocoa spills over, marshmallows afloat,
The magic of moments makes us all gloat!

Echoes of laughter ring through the night,
Chasing the cat in the dim, twinkling light,
December embraces, with warmth and good cheer,
Each silly adventure makes memories dear!

Festive Secrets Between the Shadows

Elves peeking out, oh what a sight,
Hiding the gifts, laughing in delight.
Santa's got cookies, but did he miss?
Rudolph's still munching, oh what a bliss!

Tinsel all tangled, it's quite a show,
Cats are on patrol, stealing the glow.
Presents piled high, but who's the sneaky thief?
Did someone wrap socks? That's pure disbelief!

Whispers of mischief, lighthearted chats,
Reindeer in pajamas, how about that?
A snowman in shades, is it getting too bright?
The holidays here, and laughter takes flight!

So here's to the fun, with quirks galore,
Secret holiday tales, who could ask for more?
Dance with the shadows, don't be so shy,
In this festive giggle, we all soar high!

The Radiance of Togetherness

Gather 'round people, it's dinner time cheer,
Grandma's burnt turkey brings everyone near.
A toast with hot cocoa, spill a bit too,
Laughter is bubbling, oh what a view!

Socks on the floor, gifts wrapped in haste,
Oops, double the wrapping, what a fun waste!
Uncle Joe's stories are wildly amusing,
It's hard not to laugh, he's constantly cruising!

Kids swapping presents, a paper fight ends,
Tinsel in hair, it's fun with best friends.
Dancing in circles, oh what a sight,
Twinkly lights flicker, all feels too right!

Together we gather, chaos combines,
In the warmth of the season, joy brightly shines.
A riot of memories, all wrapped up tight,
This merry occasion, we share with delight!

Dreaming Under Sparkling Stars

Stars are all twinkling, a dazzling dance,
Elves in the garden, who gave them a chance?
A snowball fight breaks, giggles in the air,
Who knew they'd aim right at Dad's big hair?

Hot cocoa and marshmallows, spilling like dreams,
The dog steals the cookies, oh, tricky schemes!
With giggles and whispers, the night carries on,
What fun it is, laughing till the dawn!

Wrapping up memories, bows in a twist,
Did anyone notice? We're not on the list!
The stars shining bright seem to wink and say,
Get ready for laughter, let's play anyway!

The magic of now, of smiles that ignite,
So merrily wrapped in this festive delight.
Under the shimmer of the chill winter chill,
Together we dream, with laughter to fill!

A Celebration of Soulful Whispers

Gather your laughter, it's time for some cheer,
Whispers of joy in the chilly night air.
Mistletoes hanging, oh what a surprise,
Who will pop the question? Oh, who dares to rise?

A clumsy old Santa forgot his own sleigh,
What's in that bag? Oh, we'll find out today!
Gifts full of secrets, wrapping so bright,
Unwrapping the giggles with pure delight!

Tangled up lights make a colorful mess,
This festive season, we must be our best.
Grandpa's old jokes, somehow still make us laugh,
His dance moves alone deserve a gold plaque!

So join in the fun, let your spirit unwind,
With each silly story, sweet memories we find.
A celebration of whispers, of joyous embrace,
In the glow of our hearts, we've found our true place!

Hearthside Reflections of Yuletide

The cat sits proud, surveying the scene,
With tinsel tangled, she thinks she's queen.
Cookies left out, a plate full of crumbs,
Santa's on time, just hope he can hum.

The stockings all stuffed, with goodies and toys,
But one's filled with socks, oh what a ploys!
A fire that crackles with warmth and delight,
While dad's snoring loudly, half asleep at night.

Laughter erupts as we sip cocoa sweet,
Uncle Joe's dancing like he's on his feet.
Grandma's old stories bring giggles and grins,
As we roll on the floor with cheer that begins.

The tree sways gently, it's shaking a bit,
With ornaments dangling, some quite a hit.
A holiday charm, with moments that glow,
Let's cherish the chaos, and let our hearts grow.

The Glimmering Promise of Tomorrow

Lights twinkle bright, like stars in the night,
Where snacks are abundant, a glorious sight.
Mom declares diets are shelved for the day,
As we munch on cookies, in every array.

The little ones giggle, their eyes filled with glee,
While trying to sneak in a candy or three.
Uncle Fred's story gets wilder each time,
With each exaggerated, hilarious rhyme.

Ribbons are sticking to every kid's face,
As they unwrap gifts with a raucous embrace.
An elf with a giggle, who forgot his own hat,
Is stuck in the lights—now how about that?

Tomorrow will come with its own little gifts,
But for now, let's savor the joy of the lift.
With laughs and with joy, we dance in the cheer,
While the magic of now holds our loved ones so near.

A Symphony of Sounds in the Holiday Air

Jingle bells ring, but the dog starts to bark,
He thinks all the singing is something quite stark.
The kids clap along to a tune that we know,
As dad's off-key singing steals all of the show.

The oven is humming a sweet little tune,
While mom yells for silence, it's way past noon.
Laughter erupts at the sound of the roast,
As the turkey collapses, we laugh like a ghost.

Outside, the snowflakes create a soft sound,
While carolers croon as they wander around.
The doorbell is ringing, it's Auntie and Pete,
With their mismatched sweaters, they're such a fun treat.

In this festive frenzy, the music does play,
With laughter and love lighting up the gray.
A symphony plays in our hearts full of cheer,
And we dance with the sounds, holding all we hold dear.

Wishes Adorned with Pine and Joy

Under the branches, the gifts seem to tease,
While the dog's out to find a new place to sneeze.
The kids are all whispering secrets so sweet,
While the cat plots a heist of the leftover treats.

With wishes adorned, like snowflakes that spin,
We gather together to share and to grin.
A circle of hope, as our hearts intertwine,
Spreading cheer all around with each festive sign.

The dinner is served with a side of delight,
As Uncle Lou's stories go deep into night.
In the middle of laughter, a pie takes a fall,
While we dodge flying crumbs as it splats down the hall.

With wishes that bounce like the sounds of our cheer,
Wrapped in the warmth that we share every year.
So let's raise a toast to the joy that we bring,
And dance with the dreams that the holiday sing.

A Tapestry of Joy and Sparkle

In the corner, the cat takes a leap,
Knocking down gifts in a pile so steep.
Wrapping paper flies through the air,
As Uncle Joe laughs, covered in bear.

A dance around, the cocoa spills wide,
Mom's Christmas sweater, a fashion faux pas pride.
The cookies are burnt, yet no one will frown,
As we all wear our festive crowns.

It's a game of charades with a bow on each head,
While Grandma's snoring is louder than said.
Laughter erupts with each silly sound,
Who knew such joy could be so profound?

So, we gather 'round with our quirks on display,
Making memories in the wackiest way.
As the lights twinkle brightly on this snowy dome,
This chaotic love feels just like home.

Secrets of the Yuletide Hearth

Grandpa's hidden stash of the good stuff,
Whispers of secrets, oh, what a bluff!
The elves are busy, or so we assume,
While the dog chases shadows around the room.

A garland of tinsel that tangles our hair,
Mom says it's part of the festive flair.
A gingerbread man dances with glee,
But he ran out of icing and now looks quite free.

The fruitcake awaits, so dense and so bright,
A weight-lifting challenge for Christmas night.
Each slice brings a giggle or two,
As we toast our success with hot cocoa brew.

Under the mistletoe, a prank's on the rise,
Siblings and cousins with mischievous eyes.
With giggles and grins, we embrace the weird,
For love is the gift that'll never be cleared.

Starlit Wishes and Glittering Hearts

The lights on the tree flicker, just a tad,
As Cousin Timmy pulls a prank that's quite rad.
With a wink and a grin, he makes a new mess,
And Aunt Millie swears it's a Christmas stress.

Jingle bells ringing, but not quite in tune,
A chorus of cats join the festive festoon.
The cookies are missing, the jar's very bare,
With crumbs on the floor suggesting a dare.

Whispers of snowflakes, all fluffy and white,
Dance through the air on this magical night.
Should we dare make snowballs and throw them inside?
The chance of a snowball fight fills us with pride.

So with laughter and cheer, we toast with a cheer,
For the holidays shine with love very near.
In each twinkling sparkle, our joys all align,
We're a goofy bunch, but life feels divine.

The Soft Glow of Childhood Wonder

A towering tree made of lights, oh so bright,
As little ones wonder, hearts dancing with delight.
With dreams of new toys and a sleigh flying high,
Their giggles echo, reaching the sky.

Elves with their shenanigans and silly old games,
Making faces, and silly new names.
Daring each other with whoopee cushions,
The laughter erupts; it's pure family functions!

The stockings are stuffed with odd bits and ends,
From last year's finds that nobody sends.
As Dad dons a hat that is far too tight,
We all start to giggle, what a goofy sight!

So let's eat again, and forget about rules,
The joy of the season makes everyone fools.
With love wrapped in laughter, the stories unfold,
In this warm little moment, each heart feels bold.

Under the Canopy of Hope and Dreams

Under twinkling lights, we gather round,
With laughter and cheer, the best gifts found.
A cat in the box, oh what a sight,
Unraveling ribbons, a festive delight.

Grandma's pink sweater, a fashion mistake,
With cookies that wobble, it's all a high stake.
Uncle Joe's snoring, a sound we all know,
While kids play in chaos, and chaos does grow.

The tree leans a bit, it's feeling the strain,
As ornaments tumble like drops of cold rain.
With joy spilling out, and a toast in the air,
It's all about moments, no moment to spare.

So raise up your cider, and give a loud cheer,
For naps and for snacks, the season is here!
With love and with laughter, let mischief take hold,
In this crazy adventure, our hearts are consoled.

Threads of Tradition Binding Together

In the attic we found, our old holiday glee,
The tinsel that's tangled, a sight strange to see.
Mom's rocking the tunes of that jolly old jig,
While dad's in the corner, just stuck on a fig.

A hat that once fit, now looks like a cap,
Worn by our dog, who's now taking a nap.
The mistletoe hangs with no one to kiss,
We'll take a cold drink and remember this bliss.

Baking with flour that coats every face,
Sprinkling joy from a sweet wooden case.
We laugh as we snack, on the dough we unroll,
With smiles that confuse, it warms every soul.

With gift tags that read, "from who knows, to who?",
We giggle as chaos uncovers its due.
The season brings joy with a dash of the wild,
In this merry old mix, we're forever a child.

Embrace the Season's Tender Light

Come gather 'round folks, the lights all aglow,
With cookies and laughter, let the good times flow.
A dance by the fire, we spin out of time,
While ants in the pants make us all feel sublime.

The snowflakes are falling, like gossip on air,
As wrapping paper's lost in the creative flair.
A solo on the kazoo makes everyone grin,
While Gramps shakes a leg, you'd think he could win.

The tree's looking sturdy, or so we all think,
Till the kitten takes flight, with a confident wink.
As we dodge all the splinters with joy ringing through,
We're trapped in our laughter, and the moment is true.

So stack all the mischief, pour drinks to the brim,
As we toast to the folly, each whim and each whim.
For joy isn't perfect, it's messy and bright,
In the glow of this season, we shine just right.

The Warmth Within the Chilling Air

Outside it is chilly, yet inside we gleam,
With the sound of our laughter, a curious dream.
The turkey is dancing, or maybe it's me,
While cousins get tangled in Christmas debris.

A hat made of tinsel, a scarf made of string,
Worn with such pride, like a funny gold ring.
We shuffle and stumble, with treats in our hands,
Planning our heists with the holiday bands.

With jingles and giggles, the night carries on,
As we trip on the lights and sing loud till the dawn.
A snowman named Bob takes a tumble, oh no!
But we're quick to recover, as laughter will flow.

So come share the warmth in this wild snowy quest,
With stories and hugs, that's what we love best.
Let whimsy and joy fill this magical air,
For moments like these are beyond all compare.

Garlanded Moments Under the Stars

Twinkling lights spark joy, so bright,
While cats chase ribbons, what a sight!
Grandma's fruitcake, oh what a treat,
Even the mice won't dare to eat.

Snowflakes float down, a dance so rare,
Uncles in sweaters, how can we bear?
Laughter erupts as we untangle strings,
Oops! There goes the dog, racing for things!

Hot cocoa spills on the tablecloth,
Silly hats worn, our faces froth.
Sibling rivalry peaks with glee,
In a snowball fight, who'll win, we'll see!

Jingle bells ringing, we sing out loud,
With mismatched socks, we're feeling proud.
In this festive chaos, love's the best,
Making garlanded moments, we are blessed.

Echoes of Laughter in the Night

The fire crackles, with warmth it glows,
Uncle Joe's jokes? Where did they go?
A prank on cousin, watch her face,
Tinsel flying, a wild race!

Christmas sweaters that clash so bright,
Sparkles and giggles fill the night.
Wrappings fly as we unwrap the past,
'Gentle', I said, but he tore fast!

Mittens for dogs, what a silly gift,
As presents topple, spirits lift.
With each echo of laughter's sound,
We find joy in the chaos around.

Under the mistletoe, a slip and a fall,
"Oh no!" someone shouts, laughter for all!
These echoes ring true, in our hearts they stay,
A night filled with joy, in the funniest way.

Tinsel Dreams and Hopeful Gleams

Sparkling tinsel drapes on the tree,
While my brother tries to climb with glee.
A noise! A crash! The ornaments roll,
Oops, that one's breakable, oh what a toll!

Sugar cookies shaped like a shoe,
Santa's in trouble; can he make do?
Nibbled corners, frosting's the game,
Whose cookie is that? No one's to blame!

A sleigh ride planned, but who's the driver?
Our neighbor's cat made a perfect diver.
Mismatched reindeer, oh what a trot,
Chasing our dreams, tangled in thought.

Hopeful gleams spark laughter and cheer,
In silly moments, we hold them dear.
Tinsel twists, creating delight,
In every misstep, we find our light.

Embracing the Spirit of Giving

Presents wrapped with bows so oddly tied,
The dog's unwrapping, now there's no pride!
Lost in the tinsel, giggles break free,
From the spirit of giving, we just can't flee.

A tree with quirks, and lights askew,
We join hands together, laughter ensues.
Every mishap becomes a sweet tale,
We're merry mischiefs on a frosty trail!

Gifts made with love, yet slightly askew,
What's in this box? Oh, a sock or two!
The essence of giving wrapped in a laugh,
Creating a memory, a wonderful path.

Embracing the joy, with hearts all aglow,
A reminder that love is the best gift to show.
While chaos surrounds with a grin and a cheer,
It's the spirit of giving that brings us near.

Illuminated Dreams of Yuletide Magic

Twinkling lights like fireflies dance,
A kitty's tail gives fate a chance.
The cookies hide while carolers sing,
Who knew that igloos could actually bling?

Mittens mismatched, a festive sight,
But who needs style when you've got delight?
Elves on the run, with tinsel in hand,
Impromptu parades—they were not planned!

Chasing snowflakes, joy on the go,
Why did my uncle wear that red faux fur bow?
With laughter and cheer, we sprawl like dough,
Marshmallows flying, sweet winter show!

Sparkling wishes float in the air,
Old socks are now gifts—just beware!
Each giggle echoes, a playful tone,
For the silly magic is ours alone!

The Heartbeat of the Season Within

A fruitcake lurks, like a friendly ghost,
Happy feet tap, while we all toast.
The snowman's scarf, it's at a strange slant,
Was it really a hat, or just my aunt's plant?

The dog in a sweater, looks so out of place,
His stance says 'Hey, give me some space!'
With joy we unwrap that curious box,
A blender for socks—who needs a fox?

A loud pop! A balloon that's been missed,
Laughter explodes—who can resist?
We fit like puzzle pieces, and what a match,
Even Grandma's knitting goes haywire, scratch!

Through festive chaos, we carry the cheer,
Even with pizza, for the festive pup's year,
We dance on the table, a wobbly song,
For in our odd hearts, we truly belong!

Glances Shared Amidst the Glow

Eyes wide with glee as we check the stash,
A gift-wrapping war with leftover trash.
The cat has claimed the finest spot,
While grandpa naps; oh, is he forgot?

Beneath the lights, we offer a toast,
To tinsel disasters we love the most!
Frog hats and reindeer, what a sight indeed,
Is that a new dance, or just Auntie's feed?

Candy canes stick, and the dog takes a lick,
While mom laughs so hard, she falls for the trick.
The tree leans right, it's a lean, mean scene,
As if it knows it's part of the routine!

With each silly moment, we form a bond,
Amidst the glow, our hearts respond.
Family and laughter, wrapped up in glee,
A wacky treasure, all for the free!

The Lullaby of Christmas Elegance

With every step, the floorboards squeak,
As we search for snacks, 'twas quite the peek!
In party hats too big—oh what a sight,
We make merry moments, all through the night.

Oh, the pudding jiggles like a dance so merry,
With cookies unguarded—oh, those will vary!
An unexplained sock, where did it get to?
It's a Christmas puzzle for just us two!

When bells start to jingle, we all will shout,
A chorus of giggles, no hint of doubt.
With lights softly twinkling, a grand review,
We embrace each odd ball, in what we should do!

So here's to the season, as we all cheer on,
With joyfully crooked tune, dusk into dawn!
We laugh 'til we cry, let the clanking ring,
For in this mad dance, the memories cling!

Hushed Moments Wrapped in Memories

In silence we gather, treasure in sight,
A cat in the shadows, pouncing with fright.
Gifts bowing gently, misplaced on the floor,
Did I just see Uncle Joe slip out the door?

The cookies are missing, the milk it is too,
Was it the reindeer or cousin Sue?
Laughter erupts, we all share a grin,
Who will confess to this holiday sin?

A tree full of baubles, some borrowed, some bought,
A leg is now wobbly, a twist in the plot.
With snowflakes that twinkle, and tinsel that clings,
Tell me again how the cat stole the strings?

Memory's dance, in a blur of delight,
Holiday moments that spark laughter bright.
We'll remember this chaos, spinning in glee,
As fun fills the air, just you wait and see!

Stories Unraveled

With giggles and tales, the night takes its time,
Was that Auntie Sally or a jingle bell crime?
The tales that she tells, so twisted and fun,
Last year claimed a penguin, this year, a gun!

A elf in the corner, he's sipping on cheer,
Did he steal from the kids? Oh dear, oh dear!
A high-pitched laugh comes from Grandma's embrace,
As she shares how she once won a dance-off with grace.

Wrapping and unwrapping, the gifts pile high,
But no one has noticed, a bear caught a spy.
He's found in pajamas, snoring away,
Dreaming of Christmas in his own silly way!

Stories we tell will echo for years,
Spiced up with laughter, and maybe some tears.
As laughter unravels in this cozy space,
We gather our memories, wrapped in warm grace.

Love's Radiance

With lights all around, our hearts start to sing,
Who left the fruitcake? I think it's a fling!
A sparkle of joy, as laughter ignites,
Love's silly dance on these festive nights.

We've hung up the goodies, a sweet little trap,
Will Santa fall for it, or take a quick nap?
The dog sneaks a cookie, he thinks it's a score,
Our laughter erupts as he begs for some more!

Beneath bright garlands, the warmth we create,
With jokes and pure love that we celebrate.
Our hearts wrapped together, we rumble and roll,
This festive connection, the glow of our soul.

Jingle bells chime with a rhythm so sweet,
As giggles and antics make our lives complete.
In this joyful radiance, we gather as one,
A family of laughter, our hearts weigh a ton!

Swirls of Frost in Holiday Mirth

Snowflakes swirling, a flurry of white,
Penguins in sweaters, what a silly sight!
We gather in circles, our noses turned red,
With frost on our cheeks, and thoughts in our head.

A snowman wobbles, his hat far too big,
He looks like my brother, after one too many gigs!
We laugh till it hurts, through the chill in the air,
As snowflakes keep falling, with whimsical flair.

Sleds tipped over, with giggles all round,
The neighbor's cat thinks it's a playground found.
In a flurry of laughter, our troubles take flight,
We dance through the frosty, enchanted night.

With love and some joy, we twirl and we spin,
Embracing the clumsiness, now let the fun begin!
Swirls of sweet memories, wrapped tight in our hearts,
Creating dear stories, where the laughter imparts.

Wishes Carved in Wooden Hearts

Wooden hearts hang, with wishes galore,
But did Aunt Pat really want one for the floor?
With twinkling eyes and a grin on her face,
She claims that she's aiming for a decorating race!

With each little ornament, a tale gets spun,
The cat on the roof thinks it's all just fun.
As laughter erupts at the sight of the tree,
An avalanche of tinsel falls flat on Aunt Bee!

Gifts piled high, and surprises galore,
But socks to my brother? I simply can't score!
"Trade winners this year," one cousin declares,
As we dive in the mountains of festive affairs.

Wishes carved brightly in hearts made of wood,
Tickling our spirits, we dance when we could.
With joy in abundance, let laughter take flight,
In this merry chaos, we cherish the night!